The Orphan & Its Relations

Elizabeth Robinson

Cover design by   Jaime Robles

Cover art by   Ralph Eugene Meatyard

Book design by   Rebecca Wolff

Published in the United States by   Fence Books
                                        Science Library 320
                                        University at Albany
                                        1400 Washington Avenue
                                        Albany, NY 12222
                                        www.fenceportal.org

Fence Books are distributed by   University Press of New England
                                        www.upne.com

and printed in Canada by   Westcan Printing Group
                                        www.westcanpg.com

Library of Congress Cataloguing in Publication Data
        Robinson, Elizabeth [1961–]
        The Orphan & Its Relations/ Elizabeth Robinson

Library of Congress Control Number: 2008934250

ISBN 1-934200-16-6
ISBN 13: 978-1-934200-16-2

FIRST EDITION

Acknowledgments

THE AUTHOR thanks the following publications and presses for having published poems, sometimes in earlier versions, in their periodicals and anthologies: *Conduit, Conjunctions, Copper Nickel, Denver Quarterly, Epoch Magazine, Fascicle,* French Broad Press, *Hotel Amerika,* Improv and Green Fuse Press, *Species, Notus, New American Writing, The New Review of Literature, Pool, Volt, Xantippe.*

Thanks to the George Eastman House, the Fraenkel Gallery (and the helpful Dan Cheek), and the estate of Ralph Eugene Meatyard for permission to use the photograph on the cover of this book.

After several vexatious years, I must also thank those whose support, intelligence, and sometimes irreverence has sustained me: George Albon, Beth Anderson, Faith Barrett, James and Jessica Belflower, Jack Collom, Patricia Dienstfrey, Susanne Dyckman, Kanga Dyckman, Karl Gartung and Anne Kingsbury, Anne Heide, Fran Herndon, Mitch Highfill, Maxine Chernoff and Paul Hoover, Fanny Howe, Colleen Lookingbill, Kim Lyons, Ken, Wilson, Jonah, Manion and Brock Morris, Rusty Morrison, Linda Norton, Ellen Orleans, Jeffrey Robinson, Joan Robinson, Jaime Robles, Laura Sims, Ed Smallfield and Valerie Coulton (with thanks for your attuned reading of this manuscript), Stacy Szymascek, Brian Teare (whose reading of this manuscript was extraordinarily helpful), Anne Waldman, and Craig Watson.

I love you all emphatically.

FENCE BOOKS are published in partnership with the University at Albany and the New York State Writers Institute, and with help from the New York State Council on the Arts and the National Endowment for the Arts.

The Orphan & Its Relations

Elizabeth Robinson

Albany, New York

Contents

Critique of the Orphan

It's not that presence is glib, but colloquial. Hear the child call,
"Look at me, Mom!"
The words reverberate across the blank playground.

The kid jumps off the swing and picks up the absence which she
then polishes on her shirt and puts in her mouth.

Whoever would have been there to say *Don't put that in your mouth*
is already in her mouth.

Plaintive: look, look.

"Look at me," says the mother who does not exist and sits like a
wad of gum in the cheek of the child.

The girl has flossy, uncombed hair. She gulps, and the gap in her
throat distends for good.

Figure and Boat
after a photograph by Ralph Eugene Meatyard

Secreted beneath, a sod house. There you sleep, shoulders curled
beneath you, shelter from the oncoming orchard. Your shoulders,
tidy and white in this shirt. You root through uneven prairie to the
house below. Invisible trees loom and compete. Who is vying for a
place to stay. Always: for orphans disguise is green. This benevolent
motion is the lie that pulls upward.

Sod orphans sleep
beneath you as shelter,

would uproot you as
disguise, white in your
effort.

Vying, benevolent
motion sends upward
the orchard.

Your shores you bury
into green, oncoming
shore
and conjoined and white
shore.

So tired   and falls flat   Or reference turns
yellow   candles under electric light

There would be no other reason   to turn one's back   on you
the viewer   who once knew   Where

all one sees now is what one imagines   the white shirt
over the strain of the body

The head bowed toward a boat that would depart

What's the use of a boat
on which is laid

provision but no solid basis

We saw all that lacked its
own premise   Food

is dead weight
when the essential

is otherwise promised
As in betrothal   The boat

sped toward the water
where its beloved

gladly drowned for want
of use   Those who are
dead and merry become food, wherefore

its lack

A boat would depart were it not so weary of the imaginative world imposed upon it.
Laid in the keel

of the boat, all those taut, looking-outward faces.

One might speak of the self without any resource for pronouns.

Someone's tampered with the landscape, only its wherewithal for floating.

On and on the story would go. The subject of the picture mutters, *Go home,* meaning, *Go to sleep,* and the hump that would be a hill discloses.

Excursion
after *The Tempest*

The boat went, then it went no more. They had set sail, met foul
weather, crashed into rocks. They

were shipwrecked as their very names would show. A violent wave
picked them from the water, then midway

repented of its action and set them gently on the ashy volcanic
sand of the shore. Natural disaster did comfort them.

A spouse, spouseless. A child, orphaned. Bound to the fury of
paradise.

Cyclicity is matter-of-fact: morning, waning of day, dark. The
orphan studies her hands as a picture of sufficiency.

Where will they go without her, paddling, plucking manna

arresting this fuzzy captivity.

And our widower watches his feet imprinting the dunes.

Catastrophe is magic. Wands bending their frond-like heads, hex-

agonal.

Old junk washes up: the consoling silence of rusted gears, plastic
produce bags.

Hands, not so far away, rinsed in the refuse. Feet, still attached to
the restive body. All rutilant, exalted at having found place

at a remove. "Abracadabra" sometime meant something specific,
was an endearment.

Survivors, the pair, gather to make a horizon. And rains come down
from the face of Caliban. Ugly monster, apostolic

in the shack of various fortune. Tides thwarted, beach effaced, they
resign themselves to a new security. They accustom themselves to
the wizardry of

apparent safety. A foundling's belief in reunion. Or
there is temporizing on the liquid face of the universe, like true
parallel lines that do eventually cross.

The ocean has swallowed its tongue.

Guilty. Named in disaster's accusation as mortal, they have to eat. Bite crust off the cosmology, barely adequate. The landscape burrows in, offers hunger as the manageable tragedy. A widening pattern of concentric circles:

there is yet little to nourish them.

A week, a month, a day, a year, a moment. Sometimes they eat impatience. The sea coughs, discharging a sense of progress, then retracts.

Brothers

If you put our names together, it spells something like "cannibal."
That's what I said to him. I would have. Then there's the other word
I didn't say. Something like "voracious." So he's gone now. One
of us is. My mother said, "You two are like those Russian nesting
dolls. There's one inside another inside another inside another
inside another."

When you are wandering and solitary, you don't think of turning back. There are concepts that become insensible of themselves. To wander is to unfurl eternally; there is no retraction.

Peculiar.

I have tattooed to myself the synonyms for "alone." To prove there is no retraction: these synonyms of the distinct congregate.

My mother wags her finger at us. Twins. She chides.

"That's the trouble. One always has to be older. You couldn't settle. How you grasped at the heel. How one held to the other."

How, now, the twin rescinds. This harvest.

You would say that I was hungry. You could say that. You could look at what I bear on the invisible road.

When I killed him, I led him. I put him inside the road inside the road inside the road inside the road, nestled.

You might memorize that my punishment is greater than I can bear. Our conjoined names. Fugitive. Cannibal.

And whoever kills me has not known the road as single.

There was no God to do it.
Someone must approve the parity that a twin is.

Memory has some relation to what I have eaten, that is, the way I have tarried here. I do not regret my brother, who is no less than myself. Embedded. But he cannot find me here.

I do, always, what I must do because I cannot undo it.

Stained Syllogism

I find myself floating face-down in the sea, and am grateful that my
hands have been bound behind my back so as not to obstruct my
view. Appalled by my nakedness, the sea batters itself with itself,
such belaboring a form of embarrassment.

You should feel no humiliation, though, to see my naked back, that
on itself frets only its gagged hands, and no other mouth. 'Soldier'
is the action that arranges flesh on a moving horizon.

I am afraid only that I might not be permitted to drown, that a
well-intentioned hand will peel my body from the liquid skin to
which it adheres. The forms of kindness flay us. Kindness, too,
being tidal; it leaves behind.

See the posture of the sea, its salt made to dissolve me. Tentacular,
the water insinuates, is my familiar, a consummation. It turns me
before your gaze, mauls my face with my face.

Mary and No Savior

Here you see me, all gold, but rubbed serenely raw so that the maroon below palpitates. At my feet there is nothing. I am absolved of history. But behind me, my ancestry grows, luxurious, a full head of hair lifted on wind.

I had wanted to give birth to an orphan, but his problems superceded mine, and history turns again. Now to work out the terms for an intimacy that can disassemble and recreate itself. Naming colors had seemed so important to establishing relation, but this comes over me vaguely. Painted over, milky, a tone and not a color. If there is not an object to love, there is still the impulse, a devotion to time itself.

Light comes from behind me, not attaching to my line of sight, but offering friction. A perverse and transparent kindness.

What lies behind me when I wake, a sort of history, the braid of bodies that engendered this self, the discord of the body's waking stretch. Even flesh is speculative. What was once skin can no longer be rubbed away, but inserts itself in one's surface like a blemish. All color revealed is a funnel pouring away what would come next, and then revolving onto the antecedents that would shape it. Doing away with sequence as well, and unfailingly.

Blue: the color unhindered space would be. History's refining abrasion.

Rabab

The walls came down. One day they fell softly. Red. Felted bricks, velvet dust. Another day their clatter shattered the eardrums of the landscape.

No one now hears her as she discerns. Discernment is an isolate art.

Penitential, she did not bathe for thirty days, then she drew the finger of her own soiled body upon itself. A perfect line marked half from forehead to groin, so that her walls were permitted to fall various: passive or cunning.

What does the color mean?

Red is not a color of indecision, it is the color of the deaf. The hue between loyalty and betrayal.

One wonders how she acquired it.

How does an isolate art get for itself the tint it needs?

Decipher.

Didn't she help the invaders? Telling them to cover their ears, tying them into the walls' delicate knots.

Bound tightly enough, the dye could not soak in thoroughly and so there were specks of the original color in every sample. How the invaders will be shoved from the top of the wall they scale, or citizens also leap as they try to get away. The gangly, natural color of them as they wriggle in the air's momentum.

The vanquishers will come. They will arrive. They will complete the imbalance.

How does one escape?
By self-division.

She discerns herself as her own sister.

She could leap from the wall of the walled city and watch herself,
alight, herself
with herself pulling apart in air, cottony.

Parity has its many kinds, like loyalty.

She covers her mouth before she coughs up a sound.

The sound, gagged, falls out of her mouth and hits the floor with a tremendous clang. The trumpets commence. The walls fall down.

In the discerning world, all walls will henceforth be red and we
will circle them.

The woman is unsure what she intended, only that she was intent.
She brings her hand down in a cutting motion, to fend off the
equal parts. Intentness, she believes, is its own material, a vehicle,
mode of surrender, mortar for the mason who scales her own walls.

Loyal to whom?

Cottony, the walls crumple. She signs them to reunite themselves.

The walls kick, swift and quiet, at her, midway between herself.

As though one eye were bloodshot and the other clear.

Inside her mind, she ties a knot and she will not let it breathe.

A suffocated knot. Wisdom,

she calls it: a red flag.

Forgiveness

Say it was a white cow and holy and in its own way interesting,
something that I loved. I have killed it, and killed it more than
I needed to. I do not need to kill it so many times or to such
an extent. It lies stiffly on its side and when I brush its hide
backwards, I feel softness. I am guilty of this. I know that when
I stop, the cow will rise, seeming unharmed. But she is grossly
injured, and I am in danger.

The Pieta of Cosme Tura

A thing that has no beauty in it should be removed. So I yanked
the rotten tooth from my mouth and threw it away.

A phantom tooth grew in its place and ached as much.

The woman sat with her skirt draped across her lap, but it was not
beautiful and when she stood, the plane of it fell into oblivion.

I believe that what I am trying to do is record a history of the scant. Record what relation beauty has to privation, scarcity, departure.

When the woman stood, I felt my body fall into the folds of hers, vanishing. Her skeleton, her tissue. I felt my body inhale the ghost she attended to.

In my theology, when one thing is taken away, another thing has the right to come in and replace it.

Not all surrogates are viable. The tooth is gone, but its substitute has been forced to stay invisible. Only the pain is real.

She has capable hands; she uses them to dust off her lap. But we know the cavity inside her.

She seems to feel my self commingling with hers. So she lifts the ghost's hand, not mine, contorted. It's ghost pain that she studies.

The phantom stands in. Creates a spectral equilibrium.

It was as if I wished to further the damage.

A prosthetic tooth in her mouth, the substitute for my mouth was the gap inside the words I might pronounce.

The sense of weight, the visual pause of her loss, draped across her lap. She surveyed it–that is, herself–where one absence is palpable and its proxy is merely a source of misery.

Recognized the injury to a body not her own.

And I covered this like a skin, no seam but in presence.

That she could ever stand again.

I would not have been an interloper if I could have avoided it.
There was the milky bit of tooth in my hand.

I had to subtract-from, which is my term of exchange. I overheard.

Substitution is the final form of beauty.

She said, "Good-bye," and the one who was gone used the same
phrase

as rejoinder.

e3

Ring and Bridge

A thing falls from its own span, but how can that be so. This would be a self watching its body's destination.

The sun, subject to demolition, loses its universality. You do not shine on me. I am betrothed only by a semi-circle that clasps my finger too hard.

The falling thing laughs at air, rapt with keeping its promise. Light falls from the bridge, sloppily, where the bridge pinches its banks, and all arguments lapse predictably.

No, the ring is an interruption of the bridge. Each is circular, like the body, at the mercy of all that it is wedded to. Circles are not, after all, infinite.

This lonely person is always interrupted. Who would not interrupt the person who says the same thing over and over? She jumps from the bridge.

I am jumping. I have jumped.

I said I was a bridge and that I could catch myself before I said it again.

A Story About Chairs

You are going away, and you sit in the chair. It holds one body, then stretches to hold two, so your partner sits down beside you. As the chair holds two bodies, it develops mechanisms for movement.
It will remove you both: marry you. It goes to the middle of the country for marriage, and this is appropriate.

One hears reference to "the heart of the country" or "the seat of the country," which terms are not as odd as they might first appear.

There's a place right under your nose where the skin meets in a seam and this proves that things join in the middle.

You stop in your daily errands, stop building boats, fixing cars, and begin to see a series of pictures flash before you. What is transportation? It's sitting still and watching a series of still pictures thrown together.

This is also what a chair is, a boat is, a movie is. Everything outside this list stops short and fuses. It becomes unified. It seems to be in motion.

If a frame is missing, it looks as though the action made a logical leap. If a frame is missing, the chair gives way.

You are sitting on the ground and the earth is orbiting, but not obviously. Once people believed that the earth was the center of the universe. Now it just circles in its accustomed route.

The loop itself has no beginning or end.

See this chair? It's a place where you may sit.
See this wooden chair? It's an object for you to dismantle and convert.

It's a piece of wood to be carved into a steering wheel.
See this: this is your durable wooden map.

It is not a chair.

A chair is a list of things. A series of chairs scattered around a house. We are empty chairs aping the shape of a body. We are dissimilar.

Then the chairs converge around the loopy heart of the table. We are plates we whisk clean. We are the motion of turning continually back on ourselves for nourishment.

In a chair you place the body of the one who is most fundamental: center. Chairs no longer exist.

You remove your loving arms to the chair. Dismantle the chair. Your legs. This is the new anatomy of motion.

Socks

I will tell on your behalf the story of a man who was lying in bed and felt a welt rise on his stomach. He wished that he could find someone who would turn on the light and write down this story for him. He remembered the day he had discovered his little daughter wearing eight pairs of socks at once. He remembered the time he had gone to visit the ocean and had taken off his shoes and socks to walk on the beach and then had thrown them into the water. Look at the waves.

Maybe I am the one who tells the story of your friend for you. He sometimes has trouble going to sleep. He lies in bed, massaging the diagonal muscle just above his groin—pronounced on men's bodies, but usually invisible on women's. Or he is fingering the sort of welts that rise on his abdomen while his body carries out the usual regenerative and digestive processes. And this is the strange thing. To know that male and female bodies are made essentially of the same parts. But when you lay them out side by side for comparison, certain qualities are plain on one and obscure on the other. And the reverse.

Then I'm a sort of tidal process for you, man whose story I tell, friend of a friend, reversal. I'm your little daughter. You are the good but inattentive father. You take me to feed stale bread to the ducks in the pond. The pond is scattered with pieces of soggy, floating bread. The ducks don't want more. So I cry because nature is against me. Out of the goodness of my heart, I wanted to feed them, but they were already fed. You make me take off all the extra pairs of socks. You might reconsider and let me keep two pairs on because I say I'm cold.

But I'm not your daughter. I'm an anonymous woman, friend of a friend. I'm recording this because on the phone the voice said, "Write for me." That's a symptom of bereftness. In an imaginary way, I'm attracted to you.

When I first learned to drive, I went to the beach with my father. I have a habit, when I go to the beach, of dipping my fingers in and tasting a little salt water. I was skirting the unpredictable pattern of the waves to keep my shoes dry. My father decided to do likewise. But all of a sudden the water washed up and immersed him to the ankles. He's so awkward on his feet. I laughed. It's the first time I ever laughed at my father regardless of his irritation.

Like you, he decided on that occasion to laugh too. I am interested in this theory of patterns. He said, "Well, the water can't leak through leather shoes." Sure it can, I think, because the incident still seems funny to me.

How ridiculous to take your daughter's clothing off her, even socks. Think of your own socks, tossed out to sea, floating somewhere or soaked through. Think of actually being a father and having been responsible, to an extent, for setting this thing in motion. It smells like salt. Salt which really hasn't got a smell, but a very distinct flavor. Or even at the pier, you breathe deeply, there are no waves, but a repeating smacking sound of water.

This is the third-hand relating of your story. There are no facts, but I include the important ideas of your being a father, a man, your sleeping body. The bulk of a huge amount of water. You've deprived your daughter of something after all. You are independent of her when you lie in your bed waiting to go to sleep. She has this idea of layers, so she cries when nature is against her and she laughs at ridiculous things.

&

String

"In a dream, I fly. It seems that it is a wedding, the opening of an event. Most of the attendants are dressed in white and mill around outside. I struggle for patience. Then I feel myself welling up from inside, rising to the branches of a tree, disentangling a strip of fabric, intending to return it as a lost object to the party. Instead, I am briefly lost in a wind, working for balance, brought above the tree, wander on a rooftop, walk back to the wedding, return the material to their thanks. The feeling of flight is always preceded by a feeling of warmth on the inner surfaces of my hands."

Randomly, god unfurls the string and pulls, propelling the body forward. Now she must get up. Safe in its socket between lip and tongue. Enamel is the purest compound she has made, a product of her own body. God ties the string to a doorknob, intending to slam. But she is up already, struggling toward the bathroom, still drowsy. And thereby saves the tooth. Coils the string back into the tooth.

"Sometimes when I wake from this dream, I consider my hands. Their smell is not human. It is papery, slightly sweet."

While she moves toward the sink, her arm considers turning on the faucet. But stops a second; there are parts of an insect behind the tap. On the gray counter these legs are orange, are well defined and muscular, and poised bodiless mid-leap.

"When I wake up, it's the cold tooth in the socket. The single nerve all wrung out. There's the cold bedroom, not very well lit. The expulsion of cold air from the wood floors and the plaster walls. Now only a tooth pulls the body forward, so that the body is a hammock for its sharpness.

There's dumbness to pain: a dog strikes the flea from his jaw, but misses and scratches his eye.

Now it's morning. And everything subsides."

In the end, you know this tooth does not incise anything. It's too weak. She told him that she dreamt she could fly and he laughed and said, "That's like a man dreaming he has the longest penis in Tulsa."

The only things lit up at night in this county are church marquees:

> No God, no peace.
> Know God, know peace.
>
> God's word is soul food.

During the drive home, in the dark, she sits in the back seat sullenly and eats the webbing out from between her fingers and toes.

"He laughed at the slogans, too, but knows better. At the tooth, trussed in its own thread. But here it is, now put in a clean dish by the sink, the orange legs still energetic, ready to go. What he remembers about my dream is the wedding and says that I want to get married. No, it was a matter of warmth and patience, held over the trees."

What does he wait for while he sits there? He should have realized
that she is tired. It is raining. His hair clings around the crown,
unattractive. At water's edge. About five inches from the line, a
frog is treading water. The frog is gray, and the rock and the water.
He goes nowhere, deliberately. He is preening the fiber of arm
and leg. He goes nowhere, soft, stable—the gray dwarfed man who
comments on water.

And she, well, she jumps in undefended. The membrane is gone
which waited for the line to pull the door open.

The Ladder

Had he, had she the sense of horizon, they would have split like a dried pod. Instead they were conjoined strangers. Two figures, unbeknownst to each other, soldered at the head, bodies angling out like a roof.

One asks the other what they might climb for. The other replies they climb like a ladder, to the height where parallels meld. And then they could go their separate ways. But they are very stable on this horizon, and in this wind.

She has seen them from a distance. Forehead to forehead, perfect in tension. The shape of the world is triangular. Her sight is opposite its sense. That they were a single enormous figure, bent double at the gut,

is irrelevant. She wants to be away from weather, and crawls into the cave of limbs.

She is drowsy, each horizon collapsing fuzzily, like a blanket.

She is on solid ground and the colossal ladder balances there, steady, weight equally on breastbone and pubis.

And there it is again, the giant hand, reaching down from the sky to take the ladder, but not from her or from the gravity she would supplant.

Rather than a hand, there was a mouth, dangling in air. She admired its symmetry. Its parts met, and split in two, and then blew themselves away.

Rather than anything else, she rose up to qualify what spilled from overhead.

One says to the other: I can see through you. Because climbing is a process so transparent.

The other one imagines falling from the ladder, and she would do it, if she could only do it by herself.

The one says: you have hurt my hip. But the other says: that is not the part that I touched. She says: I won't let go, until you tell me what part I touched. And he imagines her with a wing or a horn, another of the truer appendages.

Between each rung, the world is a different color. Space like a lens suspended. These frivolous rungs and their stains. Each color, more afraid of height than the last, deepening. Purest elevation is blue.

They are not joined. Their parts do not touch. The one most terrified defines the sky by floating.

Entrance

He has a large mouth, and he leads us to a cove or protected bay.
Where we see that the mouth has grown bigger still, betrayed by
erosion.

He is our kin and we are loyal to him.

Landscape is beside the point.

She says, "Have you ever noticed *en*trance and en*trance,* how their meanings turn into each other?"

They hesitate, barefoot, in the surf.

She makes it her project to study dilation.

The tide is wheedling, pulling sand into water, and his grin broadens.

She could be two persons at one time, as in a person's mother and a person's lover.

But he could not be multiple.

She spies on him. The way he jiggles the skin of his face, pulls at his penis, all so loose on his breadth.

Like a shore that proved, upon ultimate test, to have bones.

This is a morality play; it is preparation for departure. The 'he' and 'she' cause pain with their confusion, though it is unintentional.

On homophonic terrain, which or witch. Something trails along after them, slight but not dwindling.

While the water laps at the lips, now away and now open. One a portal and the other a spell.

Mermaid

The atmosphere overhead gives off jade salt, desiccated starfall.
Skin absorbs darkness.

Compromise, a meeting foreign to itself, below the diving light.
Her sturdy legs absorb each other, greening.

Two arms, discrete and even, bend in supplication: that straddling
by which "fuse" is both a verb and a noun.

The single green sinew of her hips. The skin on the water gives way,
a seal which narrows the silhouette, for this is the function of the
fuse, to be lit from its interior.
Scaly starlight.

Crow & Robin

Nearby, I hear the sound of wood planks clunking against
each other, and through the trees comes the clack of hammers.
Sometimes a buzz saw.

The man laughs, then says, "Have you ever murdered a man?"

His co-worker makes no reply.

The man begins to sing a song, but stops, interrupting himself with
his own laughter.

At home, I sit at the kitchen table and look out through the window at the neighbor's garden. I think about you. Rather, I imagine that I am you. What would you make of the ragged peonies, and why hasn't the neighbor cut them back as they die?

From inside your body, how do peonies smell? I am embarrassed by the limits of imagination. That is, how my desire fails as empathy and settles into voyeurism. Have you ever deadheaded a peony? I want to know not how the old velvet, browning petals feel, but how they feel to *your* fingertips.

I wonder if I'd ask a stranger, as you must ultimately be, a question arising out of genuine curiosity. I wonder if I'd dare to trespass into my neighbor's flower bed and cut down her ugly, used up flowers.

Across the street, Griffin is three and a half. He walks to the edge of the driveway holding a bouncy ball. He aims carefully and then sets the ball down to roll it.

The ball rolls evenly. Griffin's one year old sister totters carefully toward her brother on her new walking legs. The ball connects with her shins, bringing her to her knees. Her face bounces down and then off the ball.

Griffin retrieves the ball and walks back to the edge of the driveway, starting again.

"Griffin, honey," calls the babysitter, "Griffin."

Outside my window, on the second floor, two birds squabble. One is a robin and the other looks to be a crow, big and aggressive. The robin is getting beat up, but stands its ground. A huge gust of wind causes the bough to move from due north to due east. The birds rotate before my eyes, parallel with me.

The wind carries the package of itself on the arguing bird-voices until a pedestrian walks by and the crow, startled, slides off the bough and goes away.

I wanted the crow to be ashamed, to leave the branch ashamed that it had forced itself on another bird's home. Then I realize that I am the crow and you are the robin and a sense of adoration and admiration spreads through me like a new version of the weather.

The crow comes back again and again and I hear the raised voices of the birds merging with the bigger, agitated voice of the wind.

Is it really wrong to look for evidence that will prove what you want to believe anyway? I often find what I'm looking for on the chain of continuity, the leading-to or following-from. Here, in the sequence of reason, proof that things may be connected off-kilter, without our realizing the link.

This morning, as I was listening to the radio I heard this story:

A semi truck is pulling out of a gas station driveway. Just as it pulls out onto the street, a man in a wheelchair rolls in front of it and gets stuck in the grille of the truck. The truck driver drives four miles at speeds of up to fifty miles per hour, completely unaware of his front-loaded passenger. When the truck finally stops, the wheelchair is detached from the truck's grille and its occupant is unharmed. He describes the experience as "quite a ride."

Could there be more to the crow than its obnoxiousness? Doesn't it, too, have a right to be hungry, to need shelter? I watch it trying to get its glossy head into the birdfeeder meant for finches and sparrows. Very smart. If I were the stand-in for the crow, then could I convince someone to love me? I imagine watching you watch the crow, your good humor, but your sense ultimately that this bird is not subtle. A pest, you think it should blow away on a summary gust.

Coming home from work, I see my young neighbor Griffin running up the empty sidewalk looking back over his shoulder. As though, I think with amusement, there was someone following him.

I am raking up the fallen mess of leaves and sticks in the yard when I notice that the woman next door is carrying sticks and branches out to the curb. We continue without acknowledging each other. After a while, I see the man across the street sawing off a half-broken branch from a tree, and then that another neighbor is silently raking up debris from the storm.

Far down the street, some day laborers are talking animatedly in Spanish. Otherwise, there are no human voices.

In the middle of the night, I wake up to terrified screaming. One creature preys upon another. And after the screams, quite near, the wounded animal takes up a desperate snoring breathing. I turn on the porch light, and the breathing stops. Then starts again, more irregular.

I can't see what is out there, even though the sound of it is so sharp that it's in my nostrils and on my tongue. I wish you were here, to comfort me. But I make my fear correct itself: *I* would be *you,* the self at a loss. The invisible hand that rests on the shoulder of its own body, guiding it. We do not know what comfort is.

I turn off the porch light, close all windows, and make my way, deliberate, back to bed. I imagine the ragged breath. I half-dream you, getting up, making coffee, looking out at daylight. About half an hour later, three final screams just barely cut through my sleep.

I go away to a wedding, though you do not know that I am gone, and I don't want to forsake you by any admission, carrying with me what I do carry of you. A memento tucked illicit into a pocket.

I walk around the lake that adjoins my hotel. The sidewalk is covered with blots of goose shit which have baked, slick, into tar. The lake is surrounded on one curve by highway and on the other with a strip mall. A red-winged blackbird poses on a long shrub-stalk and trills at me. I fake smile at the construction workers who say hi with fake friendliness when I pass by.

Red plastic letters in block capitals stand out from a stucco wall: PHYSICIANS' MUTUAL. A nest sits neatly in the upper niche of the "H." You see what I mean, don't you? I mean, that is to say, I see what you mean. The bridge from one upright line to the next. I could have told you after all that I was going to a wedding.

Adoration and admiration for whom?

From inside your mouth, how fine to feel the tongue move against the palate and to say:

"Nothing in this world is random. Design proves its own destiny."

If I dared, your voice would sing.

Instead, I initiate the gesture forward, the bending toward. The shrub sits before you, waiting to be pruned.

Tracks

You return to a place you once lived, say, 18 North Road. You go back and sleep on the floor of your former home and eat borrowed food.

In other words: a new skin on an old thing and how certain borrowings preclude return.

The cliché example is the blur of the world as seen from the moving windows of a train. But what about the viewer who stands still to watch the train pass?

The moving air coats this lone body, unwashable afterward.

Sometimes a surface lands on a surface, a pelt on a bone.

There's a story to be told, to unearth the "true" thing. Yet landscape is still the narrative agent. You stand still, examining your hold on this: fingers wiggle.

And all around you, the grass, the road, the rails and larger woods move, making use of the language of dismay in a mouthed conversation.

Smooth but outside focus.

The surface regrets its own speed.

You couldn't get out of the way, and were struck.

And there you now have to stay, at the mercy of schedules, timetables, impact, altercations of current.

You, a static frame of bones, swept through air and restive.

A coating on history.

Chalk
in memory of Jane Arst and Joe Troxel

You never know but that death might be a sign of good fortune.
The road begins to smell chalky and shines in the dark. Up, in the
far north, darkness does not signify the end of day. But our sense
of time is put in disarray by season. You are who you have always
been, but this time, your bruised heel is glad for the relief.

You never knew how your voice acquired that wry, ironic quality
until long after it had happened. Then your vision of the divine
had passed and you had died. And people much older than you
continue to live. And your son had a child. And you stood by the
side, seasonally, and barefoot.

By that analogy, heaven is something like remotest Norway. And chalk dust silts the air with vague light. I wanted to introduce you to Joe, who can no longer see. And you lame—there would be a correspondence. But I can't breathe this stuff, the granules in all their chaotic frenzy. When you are ready to receive me, I'll arrive voiceless and I'll have only gestures.

By that analogy, heaven is a kind of asphyxia.

You have preoccupied me for so long that, in your subject, other nouns might supplant you. You as justice, or justice overturned. You as creator of the bereaved. But never you as worn out. A kind of white drape falls over your shoulders and extends along the way as you trudge, not alone: dust kicked up. That is, you concede the way as what touches you.

R-e-s-p-o-n-s-i-b-i-l-i-t-y truncates to r-e-s-p-o-n-s-e.

You can bunch the stuff up in your fingers until it becomes firmer, and all that remains is to find a surface on which to write.

I won't say that you are dying, but that you have died before the fact.

Here's a graffiti scuffed through the particulate air.

I won't say anything, because as we've already established, I'm not able.

Fence Books is an extension of *Fence*, a biannual journal of poetry, fiction, art, and criticism that has a mission to redefine the terms of accessibility by publishing challenging writing distinguished by idiosyncrasy and intelligence rather than by allegiance with camps, schools, or cliques. It is part of our press's mission to support writers who might otherwise have difficulty because their work doesn't answer to either the mainstream or to recognizable modes of experimentation.

The Motherwell Prize (formerly the Alberta Prize) is an annual series that offers publication of a first or second book of poems by a woman, as well as a one thousand dollar cash prize.

Our second prize series is the Fence Modern Poets Series. This contest is open to poets of any gender and at any stage of career, and offers a one thousand dollar cash prize in addition to book publication.

For more information about either prize, visit www.fenceportal.org, or send an SASE to: Fence Books/[Name of Prize], New Library 320, University at Albany, 1400 Washington Avenue, Albany, NY, 12222.

For more about *Fence,* visit www.fenceportal.org.

Fence Books

Motherwell Prize

Aim Straight at the Fountain And Press Vaporize	Elizabeth Marie Young
Unspoiled Air	Kaisa Ullsvik Miller

Alberta Prize

The Cow	Ariana Reines
Practice, Restraint	Laura Sims
A Magic Book	Sasha Steensen
Sky Girl	Rosemary Griggs
The Real Moon of Poetry and Other Poems	Tina Brown Celona
Zirconia	Chelsey Minnis

Fence Modern Poets Series

Star in the Eye	James Shea
Structure of the Embryonic Rat Brain	Christopher Janke
The Stupefying Flashbulbs	Daniel Brenner
Povel	Geraldine Kim
The Opening Question	Prageeta Sharma
Apprehend	Elizabeth Robinson
The Red Bird	Joyelle McSweeney

National Poetry Series

Collapsible Poetics Theater	Rodrigo Toscano

Anthologies & Critical Works

*Not for Mothers Only: Contemporary Poets on Child-Getting &
Child-Rearing*   Catherine Wagner & Rebecca Wolff, editors

Poetry

The Method	Sasha Steensen
The Orphan & Its Relations	Elizabeth Robinson
Site Acquisition	Brian Young
Rogue Hemlocks	Carl Martin
19 Names for Our Band	Jibade Khalil Huffman
Infamous Landscapes	Prageeta Sharma
Bad Bad	Chelsey Minnis
Snip Snip!	Tina Brown Celona
Yes, Master	Michael Earl Craig
Swallows	Martin Corless-Smith
Folding Ruler Star	Aaron Kunin
The Commandrine & Other Poems	Joyelle McSweeney
Macular Hole	Catherine Wagner
Nota	Martin Corless-Smith
Father of Noise	Anthony McCann
Can You Relax in My House	Michael Earl Craig
Miss America	Catherine Wagner

Fiction

Flet: A Novel	Joyelle McSweeney
The Mandarin	Aaron Kunin